Home File

A REALISTIC DECORATING GUIDE FOR REAL LIFE

Christine Dimmick

Andrews McMeel
Publishing

Kansas City

www.andrewsmcmeel.com

98 99 00 01 TWP 10 9 8 7 6 5 4 3 2 1

Library of Congress Cataloging-in-Publication Data:
Dimmick, Christine.
Home file: a realistic decorating guide for real life / Christine Dimmick.
      p.   cm.
    ISBN 0-8362-5529-1 (hardcover)
    1. Handicraft. 2. Home furnishings. 3. Interior decoration—Amateurs' manuals. I. Title
TT157.D55 1998
745.5—dc21   98-13405
            CIP

Attention schools and businesses: Andrews McMeel books are available at quantity discounts with bulk purchase for educational, business, or sales promotion use. For information, please write to: Special Sales Department, Andrews McMeel Publishing, 4520 Main Street, Kansas City, Missouri 64111.

art direction:
Guy Sealey

book design:

photography:
Mathew Zucker

Dedication:

To Grandma and Grandpa Euler

for teaching me what a real home is all about.

c   o   n   t   e

n   t   s

a c k n o w l

e d g m e n t s

Thank you Mom, Arni-Dad, and Todd for all the support you have given, and continue to give to me—and for constantly believing. To my family for all the love, laughter, and support. Thank you Guy for your exceptional design and constant patience with me. Thank you Patty for putting up with my manic panic attacks and your constant belief in the project. Thanks to Ella Stewart for introducing me to Patty and to everyone at Smallwood and Stewart for giving me a jump start on this project. Thanks to Vik Patel for all your help, kindness, and inspiration. Thanks to all my friends who let me invade their apartments—Sam, Ru, and Guy. Thank you Mathew for all your patience and beautiful photos. Thanks to all my friends at Electra. And to all the vendors, stores, and people who helped us put this book together—xoxo—you rock.

Home. It is the most important space that we occupy in our everyday schedule and it is the only place where we have total freedom to express ourselves in any shape or form.

It may be one small room, an apartment, or if you're lucky, an entire house. Whatever its size you probably eat in it, sleep in it, play in it, and maybe work in it as well. Your home is a great place, and you want it to be the vision of your dreams—even though you may move next month. When I was a kid, my favorite place to be was in a tent. I would throw blankets over tables and chairs to create my own personal home within a home. Inside I would decorate and carry on in my space without a care in the world. I loved being inside the tent because it was my personal creation. As I got older, my bedroom became this space and I created my fantasy of the ultimate teenage room. Since then, I have lived in many cities and have called many places home. No matter the size, condition, or budget (which was maybe $10), I always tried to improve it and create a special place with whatever I had.

And that is what this book is about.

No matter what your space looks like or what your budget is, you can create a space or look that is close to the dreams you have in your head. We are not looking for perfection, because perfection is limiting and boring. The information in this book is designed to be inspiration in the form of objects and materials you may never have thought of using before. And hopefully by looking through the projects, you will be inspired and come up with numerous ideas of your own. Remember, nothing is impossible to achieve; it just may be done a little differently than you imagined.

p i c k i n g

The kitchen in Beth's 1890s brick-and-clapboard farmhouse showcases such Southern primitive furnishings as a stepback cupboard that retains patches of its original blue and bittersweet paint and a mid-1800s plank-top dining table with a revolving central serving tray. The sturdy piece is set with bone-handled flatware that has been in Beth's family for three generations and copper-luster ironstone, a type of tobacco-leaf-patterned tableware that was produced in England from the 1840s through the late 19th century.

page: A Young Woman of
the Sandwich Islands, a 1778
engraving by Captain James
is flanked by leisure-
console candlesticks and
ble chestnut urns. Facing
top and bottom: In the
ning room, a chair from
eorge Smith and a 19th-
century quill, ebony, and ivory
Table. The console's Osborne
& Little cloth is accented by
an antique African textile that
de Cabral gave to Marchew.
See Resources.

Philippine Style

Modern Medley

THE AUGOUSTIN, SHE IS RIA and from the Philippines, he is Yiouri and a Greek Cypriot, live in a 1940s house on the island of Cebu, where they design a collection of furniture and accessories. "We wanted," she says, "to use all the beautiful raw materials and hand-done techniques we saw in the Art Deco period to another level." He adds: "We took the Augoustin work with natural products such as goatskin, stingray skin, wild-banana fiber, crushed shells, bamboo, and fish skin, all plentiful in the Philippines. They have also created a faux tortoiseshell print on parchment.

The furniture and accessories in the Augoustin's house on the island of Cebu were designed by the couple and crafted locally, using the natural exotic finishes the Augoustin have perfected. In the dining room, below, the chairs are covered in goatskin. The two hanging lamps are made of capiz shells. The mirrors on the wall at left have frames made from cut and sliced bamboo. "One of our creations," says Yiouri.

Tall, unadorned windows let light into the spacious living room, above. The highly polished molave hardwood floors contrast with pale furnishings that include a sofa and chairs designed by the Augoustin and made on the island. The screen is made with raffia and ginit, a fiber woven from coconut leaves. The coffee table is covered in stingray skin and the side chair in bamboo. The ceramics on the small tables and

below are by Jonathan Adler, an American artist. Sheer curtains offer a cool feeling in the bedroom, below. The console and lamp, designed by the Augoustin, show the application of exotic finishes, which also appear on their vases, bowls, and other furnishings. Ria and Yiouri, right, meet in the curving hallway that leads from the living room to the master bedroom. Their designs are available at Barneys New York.

y o u r   s t y l e

Before you start decorating, the first and most important thing you must do is decide on your personal style. Choosing your style will help you carry a theme throughout your home, give it a fluid look, and make it much easier to decorate.

Country

For some people this is very easy and for others it's like having teeth pulled. Don't get overwhelmed; there is no right and wrong, and for the most part we all incorporate many different styles in our homes. Whether your choice is antique or modern, you probably mix many different periods of each in your personal style. For example, I like an antique look, but my furniture is a mixture of store-bought items and antiques. Although the headboard on my bed is from the early 1900s and the throw pillows are 1997 Pottery Barn, they have the same style and feel to them. What's important is not *when* it was made but when it appears to have been made and that it goes with everything else.

Antique

Step #1: Research

Go to the bookstore, search through magazines and clip as many pictures as you can of what you want your dream look to be. Label it "Home File" and take it with you whenever you shop for furniture, paint, and accessories.

Modern

Eclectic

Clip out pages from magazines

and books of the look you want.

Make a "Home File" folder and

always take it with you when

you shop.

Step #2: Define Your Style

Note the overall theme of all the pictures you collected. Look at the fabrics, furniture, and clutter factors. Do you like the cluttered, romantic, gilded look of the Baroque period or do the pages you clipped look stark and clean with bold pieces of streamlined furniture? Maybe you like a combination of clean white walls with gilded gold mirrors; whatever your choice, note the details.

Step #3: Clean House

So you've noted the details, now take a look around. What doesn't go with this new dream? If your inspiration is a Victorian look, then that black lacquered entertainment center you have will probably have to go or at least be painted! Take inventory of what can be painted, reupholstered, stripped, and

saved—and what can't. Don't throw anything out just yet, unless you can afford to. The best thing to do is make a list. So you can't really turn that black lacquered entertainment center into an armoire. Write it down on your list: Look for a cabinet or table to hold the TV and stereo. Keep going until you've finished one room. When you're finished, you'll have a list of refinishing projects and new items to look for when you have a little extra money and time to spend at the flea market or furniture store. Keep it with your "Home File" and take it with you the next time you shop.

Step #4: Get Started

Now that you know what you need to throw out, look for, and redo for your dream look, go on to the next chapters for great ideas and techniques that will make this all easy!

o b j e c t s

Furniture is probably the best part of decorating and the most expensive. A couch today can cost as little as $100 (at a flea market on a lucky day) or as much as $4,000 from the J. Peterman catalog.

Trash dumpster

Of course it's very simple to furnish your apartment if you have an unlimited budget. But that's a luxury most of us do not have and it's actually not needed. At the age of twenty-eight, I have had many apartments and many different types of furniture. Many pieces have been awful and some I still have today. All were a definite attempt to achieve some sort of look that I had in my head at the time.

Flea market

After much trial, error, and unneeded expense, the following are a few tips I share from my own experiences and those of my friends. The object here is to achieve the look you want and to avoid purchasing furniture that will go into the trash with next year's spring cleaning.

Tips:

Vintage furniture store

1. Decide on the look you want. Maybe you're into '70s nouveau modern or the city-loft feel of a Pottery Barn catalog. Whichever your choice, stick with it; it is obtainable. Perhaps you'll have more pieces in the future, but you can make a simple beginning now that will still look great.

Salvation Army

The following items were found

or purchased at a flea market

or thrift store. I've indicated

their costs and resources.

Gilded mirror
$40 flea market

Old wood ladder
Free—found on the street

Wood stool
$10—flea market

Vitrine
$60—junk store

2. Refer to your "Home File"
and the pictures of what you would
buy if you were rich. Take them
with you whenever you go to a flea
market. You may not find the exact
replica of the four-poster bed you
want, but it will look pretty close
and cost a lot less.

3. Always choose quality
over quantity. This is the hardest
lesson I've had to learn. For years I
bought pressed-plywood furniture
instead of that antique dresser and
bed that I thought I couldn't afford
or find. Finally I found it at a
church sale in Manhattan. My dream
dresser and bed cost me a total of
$250; it's seventy years old, will last
another seventy years, and is exactly
what I always wanted. The pressed-
plywood furniture, however, cost me
$500 over the years and lasted two
(one year spent with the dresser

bottoms falling out).

Which leads to the next tip . . .

**4. Be patient and keep
looking.** If you're like me, you want
everything decorated in one day.
Unfortunately this attitude got me
my pressed-plywood furniture. Give
yourself a while and build gradually.
You'll end up with beautiful furniture you'll pass down to your kids
someday, and all of your friends will
compliment you on your great taste.

5. Be resourceful. Flea markets,
church bazaars, garage sales, and
your parents' basement are all great
resources. The best one of all is the
street. For whatever reason, people
throw out great stuff with their
trash. Yes, some of it is trash and
you do need to check carefully for
bugs and other strange damage, but
I have found wonderful furniture

Printing crates
Free—found on street

Metal shelves
Free—found in dumpster
(before painting)

Metal shelves
Free—found in dumpster
(after a coat
of silver spray paint)

Bird cage
Free—found on street

Winged chairs
Free—Mom's basement

Wood basket
Free—from grocery-
store trash

**China saucers used
as coasters**
eight for $3, garage sale

that people put out conveniently for my shopping enjoyment.

6. Brave the elements and holidays. Extreme weather and holidays like Christmas are a great time to go to flea markets if they're open. I bought the mirror on the previous page for only thirty dollars. No one can believe the price, but I also went out the day after an ice storm and it was ten degrees below zero out. There were only four vendors and they all wanted to go home. I didn't want to be out either and happily bought the mirror from one. In the end it actually cost me another ten dollars to get it home, but I ended up saving a lot more than if I had paid full price.

7. Look for different objects on the street. The fruit baskets your local grocer throws out every night are perfect to put dried flowers in, haul laundry, or store throw blankets. Wood flats that printers use are fabulous; stack them up, throw a few books and a picture on them and you'll have a great table. If you see it, you like it, and it's free, take it. Maybe it won't work when you get it home, but you can always put it back in the trash where you found it.

p r o j e c t s

We spend a lot of time throwing out paper. Even when we recycle, we're still throwing it out! One doesn't usually think of paper as a decorating tool because it's so flimsy.

But with the right materials paper adds wonderful texture and can make even the ugliest table look great. The following projects all use various forms of paper used in many cool and different ways. They are all very simple and inexpensive to create. While checking out your favorite stationery or art store for beautiful papers, don't forget your local hardware store for a great selection of sandpaper.

A brief disclaimer: The majority of these paper projects require the use of a spray glue called Spray Mount. It is a fantastic product for adhering items quickly. I use it all the time, but like a lot of glues and varnishes it is smelly and toxic. With proper use it will not cause any harm, but make sure you follow the directions on the can. When spraying items, always place them on a large piece of cardboard because the glue will land around your image. Try to spray outside or in a well-ventilated area. Most important, don't smoke or light any fires while spraying unless you want to become even more enlightened.

Takeout menu organizer

Take all those loose menus out of your drawers and put them into this great binder. It will make ordering in even easier.

Project # 1
Takeout Menu Organizer

Here's a great way to organize paper. Living in New York, the takeout capital of the world, I must have had fifty menus stuck inside my silverware drawer, flying out everywhere. Not anymore! Now ordering in is even easier.

Materials: One 8½" x 11" three-ring binder; pocket inserts for binder; tab separators; Kraft paper; Spray Mount; press type; and menus

Total Cost: $10

Total Time: 30 minutes

Directions: Spray the outside of your binder with Spray Mount. Place it on top of a large sheet of Kraft paper. Burnish down well and trim off the excess with an X-Acto knife. Next, apply the press type to the front. Sort your menus by cuisine, i.e., Italian, Chinese, Diners, Mexican. Create a tabbed section for each cuisine type and insert into binder. Place menus inside their proper pockets. Keep with your cookbooks on the counter or some other easy place.

Project #2
Paper Place Mats

These can easily be cleaned with a glass cleaner and soft cloth to prevent scratching the Plexiglas. However, don't stick them in the sink or dishwasher—this will ruin the paper inside.

Materials: For four place mats, you'll need eight 12" x 14" sheets of thin Plexiglas; four 12" x 14" sheets of paper or color photocopies of favorite photos, colored fabric, dried leaves, etc.; Spray Mount

Total Cost: $20

Total Time: 30 minutes

Directions: Spray Mount the backs of the photos or materials on a big piece of cardboard; lift off and place on one piece of Plexiglas as you wish to view them. Place a piece of tissue or paper on top and burnish the surface to make sure they are sticking well. Remove tissue. When all your images are pasted down, spray the entire top surface with Spray Mount and place the matching second piece of Plexiglas on top. Burnish well.

Paper place mats

These cool place mats are sturdy enough for everyday use. You only need paper and Plexiglas to make them.

Sandpaper wall border

1. Materials needed

2. Trace your design

3. Cut out your shapes

4. Spray Mount and paste on wall

Project #3
Sandpaper Wall Border

Sandpaper has a fantastic texture. This border really added to the Hamptons/beach feel my friend Guy wanted for his bedroom.

Materials: Sheets of sandpaper (try different textures and colors); cardboard or plastic template of the design or shape you want to make; X-Acto knife; cutting board; Spray Mount

Total Cost $10

Total Time: 1 hour for a whole room

Directions: Using your template, trace your design onto the sandpaper with a marker. Cut it out using a cutting board and an X-Acto knife. Spray the backs of your shapes with Spray Mount and place onto the walls. Burnish them into place, using a piece of tissue placed on top for protection (a rolling pin is great for this process).

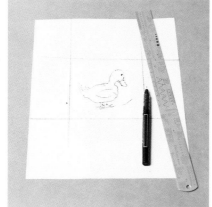

Project #4
Paper Tiles

This is great for covering up ugly tiles or adding an accent without the expense of taking out the old tiles. The varnish protects the paper and you can wipe them clean, but I wouldn't go crazy with the water because too much will cause the paper tiles to peel off.

Materials: Paper; cutting mat; X-Acto knife; ruler; water-based acrylic varnish; paint brush

Total Cost: $30

Total Time: One hour for a simple design (not including drying time)

Directions: Photocopy or color photocopy your image in scale to the size of your tiles. You can also use preprinted designs as long as they're on paper similar in thickness to copier paper. Cut the image out to the exact size of the tile using your X-Acto knife and ruler. Apply varnish to the back of the image and carefully place it over the tile you wish to cover. Burnish down well. Next, using the paint brush, apply a thin layer of acrylic varnish over the paper, being careful not to paint the uncovered tiles. Let dry and apply a second coat.

Paper tiles

1. Center your image on your tile

2. Cut out the paper tile

3. Apply acrylic varnish to the back and paste onto the wall

Project #5

Tissue Paper Tabletop

There are so many cool tissue papers available now—it's hard to just use them on gifts. This project allows you to make fantastic use of your favorite tissue paper prints throughout your home. I used my favorite tissue on an old tabletop—but you can also use this same process for a wall, picture frames, cabinets, or anything else that has a smooth surface.

Materials: Enough tissue paper to cover the tabletop surface and edges; water-based acrylic varnish; paint brush

Total Cost: $15

Total Time: 30 minutes

Directions: First clean and dry the tabletop. Next apply a generous coat of varnish to the entire top. Place a smooth piece of tissue paper on the surface, making sure the two sides of the paper line up to the edges of your tabletop. If you are also covering the sides of the tabletop, fold the tissue over them until they butt up to the edge exactly. Make sure there are no wrinkles or creases. With your brush apply another generous coat of varnish on top of the tissue. Hold the paper in position as you paint on the varnish. Smooth it around, working from the center out. The varnish acts as a glue and will adhere the tissue to the table, as well as protect it. After the first piece of tissue is covered, begin to cover the rest of the table with the remaining tissue and varnish it as well. If your tissue doesn't fit your tabletop exactly, use an X-Acto knife to trim away the excess paper after you varnish, but before it dries. After the entire surface is papered and varnished, let it dry and apply one more coat of varnish for added protection. Let the tabletop dry completely overnight before using. When needed, use a damp sponge to clean or a dry rag sprayed with furniture polish to dust.

w o o d a

n d m e t a l

This chapter is all about using everyday items in a totally different way. If you're low on cash and big on ideas, check out your local hardware store or plumbing supply company and go on a shopping spree that won't do too much damage to your wallet.

Buy only the really inexpensive stuff that comes in large quantities, like nails, and try using them to decorate a picture frame. Not everything works—but more often than not, the results are quite beautiful and even more rewarding.

Wood and metal are beautiful materials alone, but they also look fab when used together. Try putting a sheet of aluminium on a wood tabletop or a wood border around a silver door. By mixing and matching different textures, you're definitely sure to come up with something really cool and different.

Don't forget to check out garage sales or even medical supply stores for cool metal furniture, too. Not only can you get glass beaker vases, but you can also pick up an old doctor's medicine cabinet for little cash. They are made of glass and metal that's painted white. Sand off the paint with an electric sander and in a few quick minutes you'll have an amazing brushed metal cabinet that looks great in the kitchen or bathroom. Sanded metal does rust, so don't forget to add a coat of acrylic varnish on top when you're finished. If the supply of metal furniture is lacking in your neighborhood or you don't feel like sanding, buy a can of flat silver spray paint. This can turn an old almond-colored filing cabinet into a rockin' piece of office furniture in a few minutes.

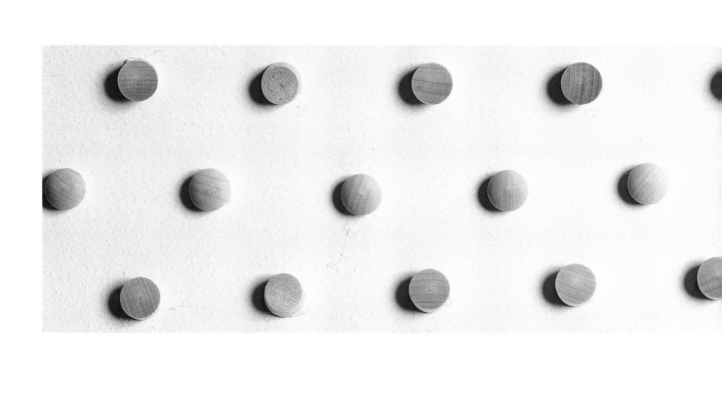

Wood nut wall borders

Project #1
Wood Nut Wall Borders

This is so simple it's scary—and the results are really beautiful. I like the wood texture best in an apartment or home that is decorated in neutral colors. The wood nuts can be substituted with metal nuts or flat-backed beads or almost anything with small, flat back surfaces.

Materials: Glue gun; wood nuts; tape; ruler

Total Time: 30 minutes for one large wall

Total Cost: $10

Directions: I usually do this by eye, because I don't have the patience to apply the tape. If you happen to have the patience or if you want a perfectly straight line, use a ruler to create a border. Start from the bottom of your wall and measure up to where you want the bottom of your border to be. Use a pencil to mark this onto the wall every foot or so. Once that's done make a straight line across the wall with masking tape, using the marks as a guide. Follow this same procedure to create the border top. Using a hot glue gun, apply a small amount of glue to the back of your wood nut—enough to act as a good adhesive, but not enough to make the glue seep out from the sides when you apply it—and then stick the nut to the wall using the tape as your guide. If you make a mistake or want to remove the nut, wait until the glue cools. It should peel right off. If your walls are painted in a color other than white, it helps to have an extra supply of paint in case you need to make any touch-ups.

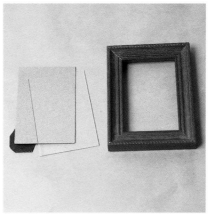

Project #2
Twig Picture Frame

This is a great way to dress up a dime-store picture frame and looks really cute with an outdoor picture displayed inside of it.

Materials: Glue gun; twigs; cheap picture frame; scissors

Total Time: 30 minutes

Total Cost: $6

Directions: You can buy the twigs at a crafts store or better yet pick them up in your backyard or a park! You'll need them in different lengths, no shorter than the longest edge of your frame, i.e., if your frame is 5" x 7", your twigs shouldn't be shorter than 7". Take the glass backing out of the frame and place it on your work surface. Using the lines where the edges of the frame meet as your guide, cut the sticks to size, working your way from the out-side edge in. The length will gradually get shorter; trim the sticks as needed. Glue each down one at a time, placing them as close to each other as possible, until one side is completed. Continue the steps on each side. Once finished, fill in any gaps. Let the frame dry for about fifteen minutes before you put your picture in it.

Twig picture frame

1. Start with a cheap frame.

2. Glue sticks to frame one side at a time.

Project #3

Dresserless Drawers as Storage

Materials: Any size drawers, depending on your storage needs

Total Cost: Free or up to $10

Total Time: 5 minutes

Directions: Not much is needed for this project, except some old dresser drawers and stuff you have no place for, like paper, clothes, desk supplies, towels, toys—anything. There's no need to buy these drawers either—go look on the street. Here in New York, people throw out dressers all the time. If you see a dresser on the street that you don't like, take the drawers instead! Or if you have an old dresser at home that you're throwing out, just keep the drawers. Once you have them at home you can paint them, stain them, or do whatever you want. The great thing about drawers is that you can put them anywhere—under the bed, on top of a desk, or next to your couch. I love stacking them in my living room with blankets and books inside.

Dresserless drawers as storage

Project #4
Window Screen
Candle Holders

One day I bought some window screen by the yard from my hardware store. I had no idea what to do with it, but it looked really cool. A few months later I was doing a project for a magazine on making candles using different elements and pulled out my window screen to play with. This project and a pillow project in the next chapter are what came about. I really love the contrast of metal against the light of the candle and the fact that it's window screen, but looks so elegant!

Materials: Window screen (check out the different types and buy it by the yard at any hardware store); candle votives; ribbon or thin wire; scissors

Total Time: 10 minutes for 1 holder

Total Cost: $2 each

Directions: If the screen is rolled, unroll it and lay it flat with something heavy on top. Once it's flattened it's easier to work with. Using your votive as a guide for size, cut out a square that will fold up around the candle about an inch. Once the square is cut out—scissors work easily on fine gauge screen—place the votive in the middle. Fold the sides up around the votive and bend the screen until the desired shape is made. To cover a pillar candle, turn it on its side and wrap the screen around it until the two edges almost meet. Mark the screen and cut the edge. The screen should be one inch less than the height of the actual candle. To keep the screen in place, weave wire or ribbon through the holes of the screen like shoelaces and tie.

Window screen candle holders

43

Project #5

Metal Dye Hurricanes

These metal tubes are old English dye drainers, which were once used to drain the dye from threads and yarn. Try finding them at your local Home Depot or flea market. I picked up my dye drainers from one of my favorite stores here in New York City, Archetique (see resource section). They are so inexpensive and the drain holes project a great pattern when illuminated with light. Try mixing in some standard pipes from your local plumbing supply company; you'll be surprised at how elegant pipes can look with just a few candles in them!

Materials: English dye drainers; metal pipes cut in various heights; pillar candles in various heights

Total Time: About 1 minute to assemble

Total Cost: $3 per pipe and candle set

Directions: Place candles inside the pipes and light. Use candles that are about two inches shorter than the height of the pipe for the best effect. Remember to let the pipe cool off before handling; the candle will warm them up.

Metal dye hurricanes

45

Project #6

Candle Wall Holder

Pottery Barn is one of my favorite places to shop and get inspiration from. Though fairly inexpensive, a lot of their items can also be re-created at home. This project is inspired from an item they sell, but if you have the time, make it yourself for less than half the price!

Materials: Metal curtain rod and holding brackets; 24-gauge wire; pliers; glass votives; tea lights

Total Time: 1 hour

Total Cost: About $30 or less

Directions: Attach the curtain rod onto the wall where you wish to hang the candles. Remember to measure the length of the wall before you buy the rod. But don't think you need to have a huge wall in order to do this project. Short rods can also look great on a narrow column or wall you don't know what to do with, like in the bathroom or an entranceway. Once your rod is up and secure, decide on the number of candle hangers you want and their lengths. Cut the wire for each of these hangers, allowing an extra ten inches for wrapping around the votive. Wrap each piece of wire around a glass votive tightly. Twist the extra wire end and wrap it around the curtain rod. Trim if needed. Repeat with each candle hanger. Insert tea lights into the votive holders.

Candle wall holder

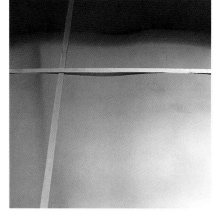

Project #7
Metal Wall Borders

This wall screen is in my friends Sam and Ruth Ann's apartment. They had a blank, curved wall that they wanted to decorate. Instead of adding pictures or another traditional accessory, I thought this border would be better. Since they already have a metal countertop in their kitchen, this wall border added to the industrial feel and gave the wall a classical modern look that goes with the style of their entire home. Check out your hardware store for different decorating possibilities like sheet metal, mesh or chicken wire, or my favorite, window screen.

Materials: Thin sheet metal; mesh or chicken wire; large rivets to secure a big surface or tacks for a smaller border; electric drill or hammer; heavy leather gloves

Total Time: 1 hour

Total Cost: $30 to $80, depending on the amount of wall space you want to cover

Directions: Have your hardware store salesperson cut the sheet metal to size for a few extra bucks. You can cut it yourself, but it's much easier to have them do it. Put the metal in place on your wall. If you have an extra person around who can help, now's the time to ask them. Have them hold the metal in place while you put in the rivets using the drill, or tack it in place with a hammer. Always keep the metal flush to the wall so it doesn't buckle. Wear gloves to avoid cutting yourself. The edges can be sharp.

Chain picture frame

1. Spray paint first.

2. Attach chain to the back with tacks.

3. Make sure the length is right before hanging.

Project #8

Chain Picture Frame

These look great hanging on a wall, but for a different look try hanging them on a doorknob, dresser drawer, or hat rack!

Materials: Picture frames in various sizes; spray paint (optional); chain link; wire cutters; tacks

Total Time: 30 minutes

Total Cost: $10 for two 5" x 7" frames

Directions: You can either spray paint the frames like I did in the photo or leave them au naturel— your choice. If you spray paint, take out the glass and back of the frame first. Let dry. Next, cut the chain to the desired length and attach it to the back of the frame with tacks, making sure they are evenly placed on both sides.

Wire napkin rings

Project #9

Wire Napkin Rings

These napkin rings look great on a modern, sparse table and go perfectly with foods like sushi. I guarantee they will become a conversation piece at dinner. Your guests will probably think you bought them at an expensive store like Barneys, but they will be dumbfounded when you tell them how you made them.

Materials:	Brass-colored scouring pad; brass wire; glass beads
Total Time:	30 minutes for four
Total Cost:	$5 for all four
Directions:	Take the scouring pad and unfold it until it's one long tube. Cut into four equal, smaller napkin rings. Depending on the size of your scouring pad, you may only get two napkin rings per pad, in which case you should buy two pads.

Using your wire as thread, sew the beads onto the rings. Since the napkin ring will lay flat, it helps to place one hand through the ring while sewing. Cut off any loose strands and carefully place the napkin inside.

f a b r i c

A lot of people stay away from fabric projects because sewing is usually involved. I'm one of them. Though I can sew, I am definitely no expert and a straight edge is about all I can handle.

Because of my self-imposed handicap, I have learned to work around my inabilities. The following projects are a result of this. In this chapter you won't find any froufrou valances or detailed bed skirts. These projects are much too difficult and take way too long. Instead I have found ways to achieve great looks with fabric with little or no sewing involved—I promise. If you can sew a straight edge you can make anything in this chapter, and if you can't sew at all, I'll show you how to do it the no-sew way.

When picking out a fabric, always check out the bargain bin and close-out sections. If you are making something that requires a minimal amount of yardage, like a pillow, this is the best place to check out first; you can find great deals.

Also look for fun and unusual materials like fake fur, burlap, and plastic. Their rise in popularity in home decorating and clothing have caused an increase in prices for these materials, but they are still pretty cheap and look really great.

And last, if you have your heart set on a really expensive fabric, always look around the store for a less costly substitute. It may not be the exact same color or pattern and it might be 50/50 instead of 100 percent cotton, but chances are it will look just as good.

These were made by gluing dried

rosebuds, lemon leaves, and fabric

flowers directly to the shades.

Clockwise from upper left:

Lemon leaf lamp shade

Fabric flower lamp shade

Terry cloth fabric lamp shade

Dried rosebud lamp shade

Project #1

Fabric Lamp Shades

This is a great way to dress up old lamp shades you can't stand anymore and a fantastic way to turn an inexpensive dime-store shade into an expensive store-bought look-alike. No sewing required—just a lamp shade, a glue gun, and a half yard of fabric!

Materials: One half yard of fabric —try using scraps from an old dress or silk shirt you don't use anymore; glue gun; scissors; inexpensive lamp shade

Total Cost: $10

Total Time: 30 minutes

Directions: Lay out your fabric on your work surface wrong-side-up. Place your lamp shade in the center of the fabric. Roll the fabric around the shade to make sure you have enough to cover it. Apply glue to the shade in one line, top to bottom, and attach one end of the fabric. Let dry. Now roll the fabric around till you meet the first glued-down end. Cut any excess fabric off with pinking shears so the second edge lays right on top of the first edge. Apply glue and let dry. You will probably have a lot of excess fabric on the top and bottom of the shade now. Trim this off with scissors allowing one inch to fold over and under the shade. Apply glue to the fabric and tuck over the edges. Finally, glue on any appliqués or beads with the glue gun. If you are using a fabric like terry cloth, you may need to apply more glue to the lamp shade for a smooth effect. However, glue will show through thinner fabrics like cotton, so in that case glue only the edges.

Project #2

Easy Tulle Curtains

I love the look of layered silk curtains—the kind you see in magazines showing a huge loft in New York City or a villa in St. Barts with the wind blowing ever so gently. Well, like the spread in the magazine, it's all an illusion. All it takes to achieve are a few tricks and knock-off fabric.

Materials: Fabric—measure from the top of your rod to the floor and add another yard if you want fabric bunched on the floor; if you sew you need a sewing machine, if you don't you need pinking shears and some ribbon.

Total Cost: $20 to $60 for two curtains, depending on the fabric and length.

Total Time: 1 hour

Directions: Choosing your fabric is the most important part of this project and the hardest—which is good and bad! You want to copy the silk fabric used in the television commercial without spending fifteen dollars a yard. Here's what you do: Go to the fabric store and check out the silk section. Find the fabrics you love, then go to the polyblend section and match the color. If your windows are small you can use china silk, which is the least expensive silk available. For one curtain, you will need enough fabric for a front panel, a back panel, and tulle to place in between them. Tulle is the same fabric used to make wedding veils; it's super-cheap and comes in great pastel colors. This is what will give the curtains their billowy look. After you buy the fabric, lay it out on a clean floor. Match the top ends to one another. The fabric should be on the top and bottom, with the tulle in the middle. First fold the top edges over three inches and iron in place. Use a low setting because the tulle will melt. This is where the curtain rod will go through. If you sew, hem the fabric together in a straight line; if not, use scissors to make evenly placed holes across the top. You'll have to press hard since you're going through six layers of fabric, but since it's so thin it won't be too difficult. To keep your hem together, string the ribbon through two of the first holes and knot, then weave the ribbon in and out of each hole and knot at the end. Then put the rod through the top and hang. Finish the bottoms by cutting across evenly with pinking shears.

HAND WASH ONLY

lili & eric
10/31/98

Project #3
Stenciled Towels & Sheets

This is a quick way to dress up plain towels and sheets. Just make copies of your favorite photos, paintings, etc., and take them to a copy store or custom T-shirt shop and ask them to apply your design to your sheets, towels, or napkins. They may give you a bit of a hard time, simply because they are used to doing T-shirts, but with a little convincing on your part they'll do it and will probably start advertising it the next week. To wash, just follow the care instructions.

Materials: Towels, sheets, pillowcases—whatever you want to transfer designs onto; black and white copies of your favorite designs.

Total Cost: $30 for a set of towels

Total Time: 10 minutes

Directions: Take to a copy store or custom T-shirt shop that makes specialty custom shirts for company events and premiums. The process is the same, except they will be applied to a sheet. The design cannot be applied to the shaggy part of towels so try it on the flat band.

Clockwise from upper left:

Stenciled hand towel

Stenciled bath towel

Stenciled pillowcase

Stenciled napkin

Project #4

Easy No-Sew Pillows

One day I went to the drugstore and found this stuff called HeatnBond® in the sewing section. It is for making quick hems, so I decided to make a pillow with it. Suddenly a process that normally took me an hour to do is now taking as little as fifteen minutes. No more loose threads everywhere or bobbin tension to mess with. Buy a roll of this and you'll be making pillows for every inch of your home. Every single pillow shown is made with an iron-on adhesive—not one stitch was sewn.

Materials: HeatnBond® or any iron-on adhesive (for pillows use the size made for pant hems —it works perfectly); fabric; tassels or ribbons for decorating; pillow fluff for stuffing; iron

Total Cost: $5 a pillow

Total Time: 15 to 30 minutes depending on the size

Directions: Cut two squares or rectangles out of your fabric for the front and back of your pillows. Place the right sides of the fabric facing each other, with the wrong sides facing out—just like you would do if you were sewing a pillow. Fold back one edge and place a strip of adhesive in between the two pieces. The adhesive should be flush with the edge of the fabric. Follow the directions on the adhesive for iron temperature and iron. My directions say 3 to 5 seconds on high to create the bond. Let cool and then do the other three sides, but leave a space on the last side to turn the pillow right-side-out. Once that's done add stuffing until full. Turn in corners and carefully add a small piece of the adhesive inside, iron down, and voilà! you have a fabulous new pillow. Add ribbons and tassels with a needle and thread if desired.

Note: The iron-on adhesive works best on cottons, silks, polyesters, or anything thin. For heavier fabrics like velvet, experiment first with a small swatch of fabric and a larger piece of adhesive. Sometimes the bond doesn't adhere if the fabric is too thick.

Footstool slipcover

Project #5

No-Sew Footstool

Slipcover

I picked up this old footstool for about twenty bucks. The fabric was a little ratty and needed to be recovered. Since the legs weren't in much better shape, I decided to cover it instead of refinishing the whole stool. It took about thirty minutes, and I can clean the cover by tossing it into the wash. This project can easily be used on a table as well; you just need more fabric.

Materials: Enough fabric to cover the entire surface of the footstool, plus an extra three inches on each side for a hem; ribbon; iron-on adhesive; iron

Total Cost: $15

Total Time: 30 minutes

Directions: Place the fabric on top of the stool so it covers all sides evenly. Pin up the sides like you would cuff a pair of pants, making sure all sides are even and almost touch the floor. Remove from the stool and make your hems using the iron-on adhesive. (Use the same method as used for the Easy No-Sew Pillows on page 63.) Once done, place the cover in position on top of the stool. Cut two holes on either corner of the fabric and thread the ribbon through. Tie a bow and trim the ribbon edges with pinking shears.

Project #6

Burlap Curtains with Shells

Burlap is a fantastic fabric to use. It has a great texture and is really cheap. The curtains shown here in my friend Guy's bedroom were made from burlap and tiny little seashells. Both go with the theme of his bedroom and the burlap adds a masculine touch—perfect for a New York City bachelor. The shells can be used on any fabric if you don't want to use burlap—try tiny glass beads as well. Instead of curtain rods, I used two doorknobs and rope. Just screw in the knobs on either side of the window and tie the rope tautly to both ends.

Materials: Burlap fabric; seashells bought or found; glue gun; pinking shears; ribbon

Total Cost: $20 for two windows

Total Time: 1 hour

Directions: Cut the fabric panels to window size using pinking shears. To make the top hem for the rope to go through, bend the fabric over three inches and cut a hole on each side. Insert ribbon into each side and tie. Add the rope or rod and hang. Once up, glue the shells to the curtain using the glue gun. If your gun has a high/low setting, set it on low. Have a piece of old cardboard handy; apply glue to the shell and place it onto the fabric, holding the cardboard behind the curtain in one hand and pressing on the shell with the other. Once the shell is on, slide the cardboard backing off before it adheres too much. Do this all over the entire curtain or create your own border or pattern.

Burlap curtains

pottery, sh

e l l s ,   a n d   g l a s s

This chapter focuses on simple ways to dress up everyday items found around the house, like glass. By adding a few borders and some beads here and there, you can turn that old, chipped glass top into something special again.

Cool items like the broken glass and marbles shown here at the left look fantastic when added to planter pots, mirrors, and even old plates or boxes. You can find almost any of these materials on the beach, at a dime store, or even on the street. Old costume jewelry is also a perfect source for beautiful baubles like bright-colored rhinestones, glass jewels, and fake pearls. If you have a broken brooch that you can't get rid of, try adding it to the lid of a jewelry box as a handle.

Never throw out a broken piece of furniture until you try covering up the cracks and crevices first. A broken mirror edge is hardly noticeable when you add a beaded border to it. Holey curtains can be fixed by gluing shells or beads over the holes. And since so many of these items look magical on their own in quantity, try throwing them in a bowl and adding a little fragrance oil to the mixture. This not only looks great but is a quick way to scent the room.

So go through your closet and pull out all those disastrous gifts and other hideous things you've received through the years and try incorporating them into one of these projects. There's still some hope for them yet.

Project #1

Easy Stained Glass Picture Frame

I picked up this kit from Plaid.® It's a stained glass kit using paint and I thought it would be perfect to cover up this hideous crystal picture frame I got four years ago as a wedding gift. Not that I have anything against crystal, but it's just not me. After playing around with the paints, I achieved as close to a venetian glass look as I'm going to get without going to Venice! And even better, I have a new frame that I love. Try looking for these paints at your local crafts store.

Materials: Old crystal or glass picture frames; mirrors, vases, or anything glass; Plaid® or any brand stained glass paint set

Total Time: 15 minutes, depending on the object being decorated

Total Cost: $15

Directions: Follow the manufacturer's directions. I recommend having a pattern in mind before decorating the glass to prevent major mistakes!

Stained glass frame

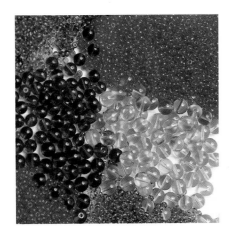

Mirror with beads

Project #2
Decorative Mirror
with Beads

This mirror was found on the street, but you can dress up any mirror or frame around the house. This is a great way to add style to a cheap, full-length dressing mirror on the back of a door.

Materials: Mirror or frame; flat-backed beads; glue gun

Total Time: 30 minutes

Total Cost: $10

Directions: Check out the bead stores in your neighborhood or the resources in the back of this book. Beads can get quite expensive and since you need a lot for this project, look for inexpensive ones in bulk. Flea markets are a great place to find unique varieties (look for chandelier pieces), and costume jewelry is perfect for this. If you have an old string of fake pearls, cut the strand and put the beads on the mirror. Try using colors that accentuate the area where it will hang. Apply the glue to the bead and then apply to the mirror. If you have a low setting on your glue gun, I recommend using it. If not, just be careful that you don't apply glue that's too hot to the mirror or glass; it can crack from the heat.

Project #3

Frosted Glass Table

My friend Gina taught me how to do this fabulous trick. It's so simple and will instantly turn any glass frosted. And the best thing is if you get tired of it, you can just peel it off. This looks amazing on old French doors and old wood-paned windows.

Materials: Glass surface; fine mist water sprayer; water; white vinegar; X-Acto knife; clear contact paper

Total Cost: $10 (not incl. table)

Total Time: 30 minutes

Directions: Tape contact paper flat onto work surface. Using a template or an idea in your head, cut out the design. Clean the glass with window cleaner and dry thoroughly. Decide on the area where you want to place the contact paper pattern or border. Spray this glass area using your spray bottle with a solution of one part vinegar and one part water. Make sure the nozzle is on fine mist and not stream. Remove the back of the contact paper and apply. The vinegar allows you to move the contact paper around and into perfect position; the water is what gives the appearance of frosted glass. Remove any air bubbles with a burnisher or small rolling pin. Wipe the surrounding area dry using a paper towel.

Note: The contact paper will come off again if saturated with water, so be careful when cleaning the glass surface in the future.

Table before

Frosted glass table

Project #4

Terra-Cotta Pots

The pots shown in the picture were all decorated using acrylic wall paint, spray paint, and decorative accessories like ribbon, moss, wheat, etc. All of the pots were old ones I had around. The directions below are for the white poem pot. All others are just as simple and require only a glue gun and a little extra time. If you have kids or are baby-sitting someone else's, this is a great project they will love. If you are going to glue decorations onto the pot, make sure an adult uses the glue gun.

Materials: Terra-cotta pots; paint; brush; thin black permanent marker; a favorite poem

Total Time: 15 to 30 minutes

Total Cost: $5 to $7

Directions: Clean and wash the pot if it's old. Let dry thoroughly. Paint the pot white and let it dry completely. Once dry, carefully copy the poem onto the pot with a pen. Dramatize your writing and accentuate the curves and loops. Let the ink set a few hours before planting.

Terra-cotta pots

Project #5
Porcelain Bead
Napkin Rings

Any type of bead can be used to make these napkin rings. They take about five minutes each to create and make fabulous additions to the dinner table or a perfect hostess gift.

Materials: Beads; 18-gauge wire; small needle-nose pliers; ribbon

Total Time: 5 minutes each

Total Cost: $2 per napkin ring

Directions: String the wire through the beads. After about ten beads, bend the wire into a ring shape to see if you need more or less. Allow one inch of extra wire to secure together. Once completed, cut the wire and twist both ends together. Using your pliers, bend the wire around itself so it stays flat on the ring. Clip off any excess. To cover exposed wire, wrap ribbon around and knot. Trim ribbon edges.

**Porcelain bead
napkin rings**

Project #6

Seashell Lights

    I first saw this idea at my friend Carol Perkins's loft here in New York. She's from Florida and when she goes down to visit her parents, they go shelling. Carol had this great idea to make lights from the shells and string them up all around the ceilings of her home. They look so cool and she graciously allowed me to use her idea for this book. The lights I used for this project were 50 percent off after Christmas. If you have an extra strand in a box somewhere, just use those. I used the indoor type. If you plan to have these for an outdoor party, make sure you buy the kind that can be used outside.

Materials: Small to medium white scallop shells; Christmas lights; glue gun

Total Time: 30 minutes

Total Cost: $5 if you find your own shells; $10 if you buy them

Directions: Add a small amount of glue to the inside bottom of the shell. Apply the plastic casing of the base of the light to the shell and let dry until hard. Repeat on all lights. To hang, drape around a curtain rod, or use small tacks to hang the wire on a wall. Use an extension cord to plug in.

Seashell lights

Shell soap holders

Shell wall borders

Shell candle holders

Project #7

More Uses for shells

Here are a few great projects for all those shells you picked up at the beach and don't know what to do with.

Materials:	Extra shells
Total Time:	Under 10 minutes
Total Cost:	$0 to $5

Shell Soap Holder

Use a large clam shell to hold a pretty soap on your bathroom sink. Look for a shell that has nice coloring on the inside. The shell is the perfect depth to hold extra water collected by the soap and is easy to clean.

Shell Candle Holders

Next time you have an outdoor or indoor summer party, place a couple of votives inside a large

clam shell. Remove the metal casing and place inside the center of the shell, with a little bit of sand surrounding it. It will hold the melted wax and after it cools you can reuse it. If it melts too much the sand will absorb the wax and extinguish the flame. This is a fast and cheap way to decorate a table.

Shell Wall Borders

Follow the directions for the Wood Nut Wall Borders on page 37 and just use shells. This looks gorgeous in a bathroom.

p a i n t

Anyone who has ever spent time in a room that someone haphazardly painted bright red knows that color can dramatically change the feel of the space.

Paint is one of the simplest decorating mediums you can use to make a huge difference in your space, but it can also be the most difficult to choose. My advice is to start simple and light. A pale yellow-brown may look just okay on a paint chip in the hardware store, but it can be stunning when used in a room that receives afternoon sun. There are so many colors to choose from now so explore to your heart's content. And though I have seen red rooms done well I suggest trying one wall first when using dark colors and living with it for a while. You may find one wall is just enough.

Painting tips:

1. Always use a tarp or masking tape to protect surfaces you don't want painted. It may add extra time but it is well worth it in the end.

2. Though it's almost impossible to clean, I find flat paint is much more aesthetically pleasing than glossy. I use it in rooms like the bedroom and living room, which don't get too dirty. Try using an eggshell paint for the kitchen or the bathroom. It has the slightest bit of gloss to it and can be easily

cleaned with a sponge. Also check out scrubbable flat paint. This has the look of flat paint, but it can also be washed.

3. If you are working with a color other than a shade of white, I recommend buying a small amount (quart) of the color first and testing it on the walls in the room you are painting, before spending money on gallons. While working on this book, I repainted my home. To save money I ventured out to Brooklyn's Home Depot. Looking at the paint chips inside the store, I picked out what I thought to be the perfect shade of celery green. Since I was there to save money and was using a borrowed car to bring it all back, I bought all six gallons that I needed. When I got home and tested the walls with the paint, the beautiful celery green turned into a hideous electric green. Instead of saving money, I ended up buying another six gallons here in Manhattan. So even when

you think you are sure, always test before buying.

4. Always check the color of your test spot in both daylight and night light. There is a dramatic difference in the colors when using something other than white. If your apartment receives a lot of light, go with the color that looks best then and vice versa.

5. Paint swatches are like free candy—let yourself pick whatever you want and take them home. Once home, tape them to your walls, checking the color in daylight and at night. This will help you decide which color you should test with.

6. Unless your apartment is a museum, there is no need to spend a fortune on high-cost paints. I'm not suggesting you go with the cheapest brand, but a medium-priced paint on sale will do just fine. Benjamin

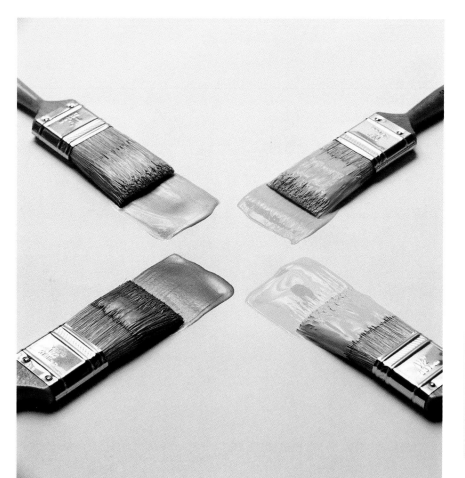

Just painted

24 hours later

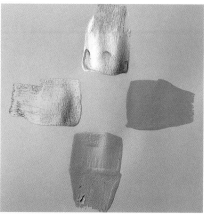

Moore, Janovic Plaza House Brand, and Martha Stewart's Kmart brand paint are all good choices and come in a wide variety of colors.

7. Always keep an extra amount of paint in an airtight jar handy, before putting the rest in the basement or storage. I use old, clean pasta-sauce jars. Mark the paint color on the outside with masking tape. You can shake them easily and the paint doesn't dry out. These come in handy for quick touch-ups on marked walls. I just put a little on a paper towel and wipe the wall with it. Once dry you can't tell the difference.

8. Choose colors in the same family. If you're using a cream color paint that has a lot of yellow in it, make sure the second color you use is also yellow-based.

9. There are many theories on this, but in my opinion paint dries darker than the swatch—or maybe it just looks darker because the swatch is so small. Whatever it is, if you are unsure about the strength of the color, it is always safer to go with the lighter color.

10. If you make a mistake, don't stress over it; you can always paint over it!

Project #1
Painting over Eyesores

Never let an ugly wall get you down. If you can't work with the style of it, paint can do wonders. It's always worth a try. In my old office we had '70s wood paneling everywhere. Though I could've worked a retro style into the office, I didn't because the reoccurrence of bell-bottoms is just about enough '70s for me. The thought of pulling down all that paneling was a little much and covering the walls in fabric would be too expensive—so I decided to paint. The results created a world of difference. Instead of the basement of the *Brady Bunch* house, the walls turned into a clapboard beach house in the Hamptons. I used two coats of a light pastel paint and no primer. Primer was recommended to me at the paint store as a necessary item to adhere the paint to the paneling. I didn't use it because

I didn't have the extra time or money. Now I don't normally go against the advice of experienced painters, but in this case I took a chance and it worked. If you are considering painting over wood paneling in your home, test a small area with two coats first to see if the primer is needed—before you take my advice!

Materials: Flat antique white paint or pale-color paint; paint roller; primer if needed

Total Time: 2 hours for an 8' x 12' room

Total Cost: $30

Directions: Clean the walls first with a mild soap and water. Let dry. Remove any protruding nails or items stuck on the paneling. Paint one coat and then immediately do the second coat. If you are using a primer, let it dry before painting.

Before

After

Before antiquing walls

After antiquing walls

Project #2
Antiquing Damaged Walls

Though most people would never buy or rent a home with damaged walls such as these, in New York City it's a much different story. The walls shown here are in my friend Zaldy's apartment at the Chelsea Hotel. The Chelsea is a fantastic old building with many stories. Sid Vicious, Edie Sedgewick, and Dylan Thomas are just a few of its famous residents. Zaldy is a fashion designer and he uses the space as a studio and living area. Since he makes a lot of messes and pays a lot in rent, he didn't want to spend more of his own money on repairs, which would be significant in cost. Instead of covering up the walls, we decided to work with cracks and holes. With a few simple paint techniques, we managed to turn the old walls into something you might find in an old village in Italy or Greece. It saved a ton of money and added even more character to his home.

Materials: Flat paint; tinting in a shade darker and lighter than the paint; water-based glaze; paint roller; rag for glazing; two to three old plastic containers

Total Time: 1 hour for one 8' x 10' wall

Total Cost: $20

Directions: First paint the entire wall in the color you want. Yellows look great with this technique and really warm up the wall, but any color can be used. Once dry, it's time to add the color and dimension. Using your plastic containers, pour a little bit of glaze into each. Now add a little tint to each one and stir. What you are trying to do is create a few slightly different shades of the paint. You do not want a drastic difference. Think of a colored wall that is sunny and shaded at the same time. Though it is the same color all over, the lighting creates different shades on it. Once you have your different shades mixed, apply a little to the wall with a damp rag, working in sweeping motions with your hands. Start at the bottom first, so as you get comfortable with the process you work your way up. When I did this I used the crevices and cracks as a guideline, darker in the crevices, lighter around them, etc. Think of a beautiful painting and you will do fine. The glaze does dry quickly, so you need to work fast. If you're nervous, try practicing on a piece of white mechanical board from your local art store first to increase your confidence—once you get the hang of it it's as easy as finger painting!

Unpainted tiles

Painted tiles

Project #3
Painting over Tiles

This is a great way to cover up ugly colored tiles in a bathroom. There are drawbacks though—the paint really smells and you can't use the bathroom for three days. But it is a lot easier than retiling!

Materials:	Epoxy paint and brushes; work gloves; face mask; lots of ventilation; (if your bathroom does not have any windows, I recommend doing a small area at a time over a few weeks)
Total Time:	1 hour
Total Cost:	$20
Directions:	Carefully follow the directions on the epoxy paint.

Always wear a face mask and protective gloves and clothing. Keep all pets and children away for this process.

Chalkboard bulletin board

Project #4
Chalkboard Bulletin Board

Crayola® makes this fantastic paint now called chalkboard paint. You can paint it on walls, tables, or anything and they will instantly turn into a chalkboard surface when dry. I painted over a bulletin board for this project, giving it a dual use. If you have kids, it might be fun to paint a closet door for them.

hang the board, you can either use nails or take a long ribbon and staple it to the back of the board with a heavy-duty staple gun. Position each end a few inches from the corners so it will hang balanced.

To erase the chalkboard messages, you can use a chalkboard eraser or a wet sponge.

Materials: Bulletin board; Crayola® chalkboard paint; brush; silver spray paint; ribbon

Total Cost: $12

Total Time: 30 minutes

Directions: First spray paint the natural wood of the frame with a flat silver spray paint and let it dry. Then paint the bulletin board surface with the chalkboard paint; at least two coats will be needed. To

Project #5

Spray Paint Frames

Gold and silver spray paint are two of my favorite ways to spruce up anything. Here I did a whole bunch of frames I bought at a dime store—three for five dollars. The spray paint hides their cheapness and makes them elegant enough to put on any wall. Just get a whole bunch of different sizes in the same shape for the look pictured here.

Materials: Cheap wood picture frames; silver and gold flat spray paint

Total Time: 10 minutes for each frame

Total Cost: $2 to $3 a frame

Directions: Take out the glass from the frames and spray paint them outside using a large piece of cardboard to catch the excess paint. Make sure you get the sides and corners sprayed. Let dry thoroughly before inserting the pictures.

Spray paint frames

a n d   s c e n t s

Scenting your home is one of the easiest ways you can personal-
ize it. Think about when you walk into a friend's home that
smells great. Before you even notice the decor, you want to
know what the wonderful smell is.

I work with and create new scents every day at my company and have tried and tested many ways to use them throughout a home. Some ideas failed miserably, but others, like our candles, have met with great success. The one thing I have learned is that scent is very personal. While some love our jasmine-scented candles, it's too strong for others. Since it is your home, the smell and its strength are your choice. Try mixing scents and work with the smells of the season, like orange and pine for Christmas. Either essential oils or potpourri oils can be used unless otherwise indicated.

Project #1

Quick and Easy Flower Arrangements

Flowers are a wonderful way to bring scent into your home while making it look great at the same time. Here are a few quick tips and ideas for arrangements:

1. Use out-of-the ordinary containers for vases. Old glass jars and tin cans that once contained pickles, spaghetti sauce, or peas are great for quick arrangements. Check out flea markets for antiques.

2. Always keep leaves out of the water to prevent it from smelling bad and turning brown. If you use a weedy flower like cornflowers, add a teaspoon of bleach to the water to keep it from turning quickly.

3. Always cut the stems of flowers before putting them in water, even if you just got them from the florist. Warm water will open up the flower buds quickly, cool water will keep a bloomed flower longer.

4. Expensive flowers like Casablanca lilies and orchids look great even if there is only one stem. Cheaper flowers like daisies look best when a ton are bunched together.

5. Always hold the arrangement in one hand, while using your other to create it. When it's all bunched together and looks great, hold it up next to the vase for height to tell where the stems should be cut.

6. Don't combine carnations or baby's breath with any flower arrangement. The arrangement will look better without them.

7. Add cool-looking rocks, shells, or cranberries to the bottom of a clear vase for a neat look.

8. Keep a pair of scissors specifically for cutting the stems; if you use the same scissors for fabric, the flower cutting will eventually ruin them.

9. Change the water and re-cut the flowers every three days to help them last longer.

10. Use dried rosebuds and petals for plant potpourri. Just snip off the heads when done and toss them onto a big potted plant. They look pretty and will keep the soil moist so you don't have to water them as much.

Project #2

Living Wreath

These wreaths are perfect for a party, wedding, bridal shower, baby shower—it's endless. They look gorgeous on the door and smell great. Try using one specific flower for a holiday, like poinsettia leaves for Christmas; it's really stunning and you can use anything that has a strong stem. I recommend placing one on a door or using one as a centerpiece for a table. The wreath needs to be moist to keep the flowers alive, but it can drip, so don't put it on a wall inside, unless you cover the back with plastic. With daily sprayings, this wreath will last one week.

Materials: Two metal wreath frames of the same size; 24-gauge floral wire; one chopstick; florist's foam oasis in green; enough sheet moss to cover the front and back of your frame; dull knife; ribbon; flowers with a strong stem (lilies, roses, hydrangeas, daisies, tulips)

Total Time: 1 hour

Total Cost: $35 (using regular white lilies)

Directions: Place one wreath frame wrong-side-up on your work table. Using the dull knife, cut the oasis into thick slices and place firmly into the wreath base. Do this around the entire frame, filling in every crack with oasis. You want the oasis to stick out above the frame, because you will be putting the other frame on top like a sandwich. Once the frame is filled, place the second frame on top, right side up. Wrap wire around the entire wreath and tie securely. Now place the wreath in the sink and thoroughly soak it. This will take awhile; the oasis holds a lot of water. Once this is done, begin wrapping the moss around the wreath with the wire until the front and back are completely covered. Now tie the ribbon securely in a knot and create a strong hanger for the wreath. When that is completed you can begin inserting the flowers. Using the chopstick, poke into the wreath to create a deep hole for the stem. Cut the flower leaving a $1^{1}/_{2}$" inch stem. Gently push the stem into the hole and continue the process all around the wreath. If placed on a surface that can be damaged by water, put a protective surface underneath it first.

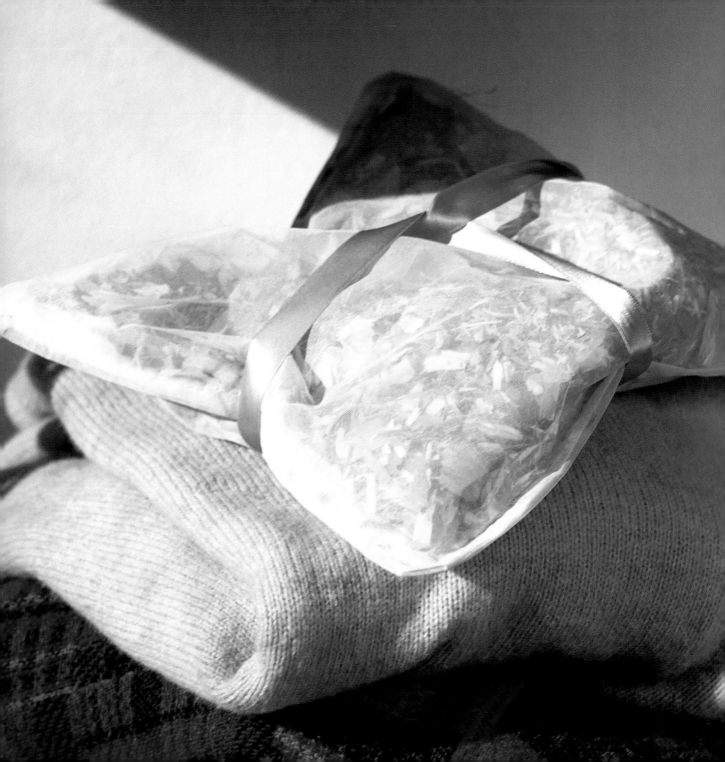

Project #3

Cedar Closet Sachets

These look great and keep the moths from eating your favortie sweaters.

Materials: Cedar chip bedding from any pet supply store; 1/2 yard of fabric; ribbon; iron-on adhesive (hem width); iron

Total Time: 15 minutes

Total Cost: $8 for four sachets

Directions: Cut out the material for the two sides of your sachet and, using the iron-on adhesive, seam the pillow on all three sides. Leave the fourth side one-quarter open. Turn the sachet inside out and stuff with cedar chips. Seal the open corner shut with the iron-on adhesive and decorate with a ribbon bow. Place it in your closet, a trunk, or hang inside a closet on the clothing rod. To replenish the cedar scent, add a few drops of essential oil of cedar when needed.

Cedar closet sachets

Glass potpourri

Tree potpourri

Scented candles

Project #4
Broken Glass Potpourri

Living in New York City, I often find shattered glass on the street. If car break-ins are not a regular occurrence in your town, check your auto shop for some glass. They may look at you strangely, but they'll probably give it to you for free! If you have pets or children, do not do this project. They will be far too interested in the glass and may eat it. Try using found shells or rocks instead.

Materials: Scented oil; broken glass; cool jar to put it in

Total Time: 5 minutes

Total Cost: $3

Directions: Carefully scoop up the glass using old work gloves. Place the glass in the jar, add a tablespoon of scented oil, and mix well.

Project #5
Quick Scents for Any Room

Here are a few quick ways to scent your apartment inexpensively.

1. Spray your bedsheets with a favorite perfume for sweet dreams.

2. Place potpourri on top of your large potted plants to scent your entire home.

3. Scented candles work wonders; the more expensive they are the stronger the scent in your home because there is more oil added to them. Glue fragrant bay leaves around the candle for a unique look.

4. Wrap some potpourri up tightly in a muslin bag and throw it in the dryer with your wet clothes to scent your laundry.

5. Place unwrapped scented soaps in a basket in the bathroom; the moisture brings out the scent when you bathe.

Project #6
Table Trees

I keep these around the house year-round. Try big flowers like dried marigolds for a fun look.

Materials: Terra-cotta pot; stick; foam tree form; dried sheet moss; dried flowers; glue gun; plaster of paris

Total Time: 1 hour

Total Cost: $10

Directions: Wrap the moss around your tree form using glue or floral wire. Place one end of the stick into the bottom of your tree, like a trunk. Prepare the plaster of paris and pour it into the pot; immediately place the bottom of the tree's trunk into the plaster. Hold it there or place tall books around it to hold the tree in place until hardened. Once completely hardened, begin decorating, working from the bottom up. When done, scent the tree with your favorite oil.

Table trees

Pomander ball

Project #7
Pomander Balls

My company makes these and I keep a ton on my doorknobs and inside closets.

Materials: Styrofoam ball any size; ribbon; glue gun; dried flowers or peas; beans; bay leaves; star anise

Total Time: 40 minutes

Total Cost: $8

Directions: Loop a piece of ribbon and glue it to the Styrofoam ball to create a hanger. Imagine the ball as an orange in four equal sections. Apply a row of flowers starting at the top of the ribbon and making a straight line down to the bottom. Do another row to create the illusion of a quarter of an orange. Once done, fill in that section and move to the next quarter. When that's completed, half of the ball will be covered and one half will not. Make a row down the middle of the empty half, creating two sections and fill each one in. Though you do not have to decorate your ball by quarter sections, this does help give it an overall symmetrical look. When finished scent with your favorite oil.

Mini Glossary of Terms

Acrylic Varnish:
A water-based varnish that provides a clear protective coating. Found at most hardware and any art stores.

Batting:
A flat stuffing made of polyester or natural fibers used to add loft or padding to chairs, couches, or foot stools.

Bias:
A line diagonal to the grain of fabric.

Burnisher:
An artist's tool used to smooth down surfaces. Found at any art supply store.

Contact Paper:
A self-adhesive paper traditionally used to cover the insides of cupboards and drawers. Mostly available in pattern prints.

Cornice:
A wood frame, often covered with fabric, mounted at the top of draperies or horizontal molding at the top of a wall.

Epoxy Paint:
A paint with a synthetic adhesive used on tiles and bathtubs. Always use in a well-ventilated area and away from flames.

Fiberfill:
Pillow fluff—a synthetic filling used in pillows and couches.

French Door:
A door with rectangular panes extending its full length.

Glaze:
Available in water or oil base. Use to add shine or mix with tints for special painting effects.

ate guide

Grain:
The direction in which the fabric fibers or wood fibers run.

Hem:
An edge of cloth folded over and sewn across.

Iron-on Adhesive:
A fusible tapelike substance that bonds fabric together when heated. Also called fusible bonding. HeatnBond® is the brand name of a fusible web.

Latex Paint:
Water-based paint used for most interior painting jobs.

Primer:
A base applied to walls and wood to aid in adhering paint.

Flat Finish:
Dull with no shine

Gloss:
High-shine finish

Semigloss:
Shiny finish

Eggshell:
Slight gloss finish

Shirr:
A method by which fabric is gathered.

Spray Mount:
An aerosol spray glue. Found at any art supply store. Always use in a well-ventilated area and away from flames.

Swag:
A draping of fabric at the top of curtains.

Tiebacks:
Fabric, rope, or ribbon that holds curtains open.

Household Measurements

Flat Sheets

Twin
66" x 96"

Double/Full
81" x 96"

Queen
90" x 102"

King
108" x 102"

Pillowcases and Shams

Standard Pillowcase
20" x 30"

King Pillowcase
20" x 40"

European Sham
26" x 26"

Beds

Twin
39" x 75"

Double/Full
54" x 75"

Queen
60" x 80"

King
76" x 80"

Food Weights and Measurements

3 Teaspoons = 1 Tablespoon

4 Tablespoons = ¹/₄ Cup

5¹/₃ Tablespoons = ¹/₃ Cup

8 Tablespoons = ¹/₂ Cup
12 Tablespoons = ³/₄ Cup

16 Tablespoons = 1 Cup

2 Tablespoons = 1 Fluid Ounce

1 Cup = 8 Fluid Ounces

1 Cup = ¹/₂ Pint

4 Cups = 1 Quart

8 Cups = ¹/₂ Gallon

16 Cups = 1 Gallon

128 Fluid Ounces = 1 Gallon

Square Footage = length x width
i.e., a 10' x 10' room is 100
square feet

1 gallon of paint will cover
400 sq. feet (one coat)

12 Inches = 1 Foot
36 Inches = 1 Yard

" = Inches

' = Foot

Stains, Remedies, and Cleaning Tips

Freezer:
To clean the inside make a paste of baking soda and water. Scrub with a damp sponge.

Greasy Countertops:
Wipe away excess with a paper towel. Use rubbing alcohol to remove any additional residue. Clean again with a sponge. If you have a gloss finish on your countertop, do not use this method!

Stuck Glasses:
To separate glasses that are stuck together, place ice cubes in the top glass and put the bottom glass in hot water.

Grungy Pots and Pans:
Soak food-encrusted pans with baking soda, hot water, and soap.

Oily Bottles:
To clean the inside of an oily bottle, add two tablespoons of ammonia and fill with cold water. Close top, shake well, drain, and rinse several times with soap and water.

Tarnished Silver:
Make a paste of salt and water. Scrub with a soft cloth and rinse.

Tarnished Copper:
Add one tablespoon of salt to one lemon half and scrub. Rinse off.

Chrome Cleaner:
Use a baking soda and water paste.

Stainless Steel Polisher:
Rub with a soft rag and a little bit of baby oil.

Ink Removal:
Rub stain with milk, rinse, and wash.

Red Wine Stains:
Add stained fabric to a solution of $\frac{1}{4}$ milk to $\frac{3}{4}$ water. Bring to a boil and simmer for three to four minutes, or until stain is gone. Wash as usual.

Alcohol Stains:
Place stained fabric over a large bowl and rubber band it taut. Add salt to the stain and pour boiling water over it. Only do this on washable fabrics.

Candle Wax:
Scrape off as much wax as possible. Place the stained fabric on an ironing board or counter. Place a few layers of napkins or paper towels underneath and on top of the wax stain. Iron over the paper towels or napkins

with a high/cotton setting. The wax
will melt into the towels or tissue.
Keep adding fresh towels on top and
underneath until wax is removed.
Wash as usual.

Blood Stains:
Scrub fresh stains with cold water and
detergent. Keep rinsing and scrubbing
until removed. On old blood stains
add a few drops of diluted ammonia
on the stain and then wash. Only do
this on washable fabrics.

Makeup Stains:
Add detergent to stain and wash as
usual. Only do this on washable fabrics.

Coffee or Tea:
Stretch and fasten stained fabric over
a bowl. Pour hot water over stain.
Only do this on washable fabrics.

Chocolate:
Soak in cold water for 45 minutes or
more. Scrub stain with detergent,
rinse, and wash in cold water. Only
do this on washable fabrics.

Cheap and Chic Resources

All resources listed sell to both retail and wholesale customers unless otherwise noted.

Dried Flowers, Herbs, Essential Oils, and Potpourri Oils

Atlantic Spice
P.O. Box 205
North Truro, MA 02652
1.800.316.7965
Free Catalog

San Francisco Herb Co.
250 14th St.
San Francisco, CA 94103
1.800.227.4530

B&J New York Florists' Supply Inc.
103 West 28th St.
New York, NY 10001
212.564.6086

Cool Jars, Bottles, and Cans

Freund Can Company
155 West 84th St.
Chicago, IL 60620
773.224.4230

Bowery Kitchen Supplies Chelsea Market
460 West 16th St.
New York, NY 10011
212.376.4982

Bed, Bath & Beyond
620 Ave. of the Americas
New York, NY 10011
212.255.3550

Fishs Eddy
Broadway & 19th St.
New York, NY 10010
212.420.9020

N.Y. Cake & Baking Dist.
56 West 22nd St.
New York, NY 10010
212.675.CAKE

Cheap Craft Supplies—Glue Guns, Sticks, Styrofoam Balls, Wreath Frames, and Much More

Bolek's Craft Supplies
P.O. Box 465
330 N. Tuscarawas Ave.
Dover, OH 44622
1.800.743.2723

Pearl Paint
308 Canal
New York, NY 10013
212.431.7932

Paint, Plumbing, and Hardware

Janovic Plaza
215 Seventh Ave.
New York, NY 10011
212.645.5454

Kove Hardware
189 Seventh Ave.
New York, NY 10011
212.929.4558

Plastic Beads and Baubles

York Novelty Import, Inc.
10 West 37th St.
New York, NY 10018
1.800.223.6676

Bolek's Craft Supplies
P.O. Box 465
330 N. Tuscarawas Ave.
Dover, OH 44622
1.800.743.2723

Industrial Plastics
309 Canal St.
New York, NY 10013
212.226.2010

Shells, Baskets, Terra-Cotta Pots, Dye Tubes, and Other Fascinating Items

Archetique
123 West 28th St.
New York, NY 10001
212.563.8003

Just Seashells

Seashell Warehouse
#1 Whitehead St.
Key West, FL 33040
305.294.5168

Fabric and Ribbon

Hyman Hendler & Sons
67 West 38th St.
New York, NY 10018
212.840.8393

M&J Trimmings
1008 Ave. of the Americas
New York, NY 10018
212.391.9072

Patterson Silks
36 East 14th St.
New York, NY 10003
212.WA9-7861

B&J Fabrics, Inc.
263 West 40th St.
New York, NY 10018
212.354.8150

L.P. Thur Fabrics
126 West 23rd St.
New York, NY 10011
212.243.4913

Exotic Silks
1959 Leghorn St.
Mountain View, CA 94043
800.845.SILK

B&J New York Florists' Supply Inc.
103 West 28th St.
New York, NY 10001
212.564.6086

Cheap Frames, Candles, and Tea Lights

IKEA
1000 Center Drive
Elizabeth, NJ 07202
908.289.4488

Slipcovers

Martin Albert Interiors
9 E. 19th St.
New York, NY 10003
800.525.4637

Cool Stuff and Cheap Chic for Your Home

Crate & Barrel
650 Madison Ave.
New York, NY 10022
800.323.5461

Old Navy
610 Ave. of the Americas
New York, NY 10011
212.645.0663

Fishs Eddy
Broadway & 19th St.
New York, NY 10010
212.420.9020

Housing Works Thrift Shops
143 West 17th St.
202 East 77th St.
New York, NY
212.772.8461

Williams Sonoma
Pottery Barn
Hold Everything
Outlet Centers
231 Tenth Ave.
New York, NY 10011
212.206.8118

La Maison Moderne
144 West 19th St.
New York, NY 10011
212.691.9603

Bowery Kitchen Supplies
Chelsea Market
460 West 16th St.
New York, NY
212.376.4982

Flea Market
26th & 6th Ave.
New York, NY 10011
212.243.5343

The Garage Flea Market
25th St. Btwn. 6th & 7th Ave.
New York, NY 10011
Every Sunday, morning til night

Soho Flea Market
Broadway & Grand St.
New York, NY
212.682.2000

Dish Is
143 West 22nd St.
New York, NY 10011
212.352.9051

Calvary St. George's
Vintage Furniture Store
(ask for Joe or Paul)
277 Park Ave. South
New York, NY 10010
212.475.6645

The Good Home Co.
(catalog only)
Old Chelsea Station
P.O. Box 76
New York, NY 10113-0076
1.800.GHC.2862

Paris Brooklyn
(catalog only)
118 North 11th St.
2nd Floor
Brooklyn, NY 11211
718.388.4466

The collage images
on pages 12 and 14
are from the following
magazines:
Metropolitan Home
Country Living
Elle Decor
Maire Claire Maison
Maire Claire Ideas
Victoria Magazine
Weekend Decorating
Interior Design
Thanks!

notes

notes

notes

notes

notes

notes

notes